INTRODUCTION

Whether you are viewing exhibits at the museum or camping o
woods, you can turn short trips into teaching trips just by making use of the
surroundings and ordinary items found at the site.

Teaching Trips is divided into ten chapters: Museum, Zoo, Park, Airport,
Picnic, Farm, Woods, Beach, Travel Games, and Trip Tips.

Each of the first eight chapters contains fun, easy activities to do at the
trip site, followed by related activities that you and your child can do when
you return home. A chapter of travel games provides a variety of activities to
do in the car or at the site. And a final chapter offers helpful hints for
making any outing with young children run smoothly.

The activities in the chapters are grouped into the areas of language,
creativity, thinking skills, coordination, science, and self-awareness. At first
glance, these activities might seem to be "just play." However, as the
introductory sentences to the activities explain, each utilizes a specific skill—
one that forms part of a foundation necessary for higher learning.

For instance, participating in dramatic-play and oral-language activities
prepares your child for communicating clearly with others. Art projects spark
the imagination needed for effective reading, writing, and scientific
speculation. Playing matching and sorting games develops an understanding
of likes and differences, a skill used in nearly all learning areas, including
math, science, reading, and writing. Small-muscle coordination activities
pave the way for learning how to use a pen or pencil, science activities
promote thinking skills, and self-esteem activities lead to building self-
confidence, so necessary for your child's success in all learning areas.

Since you are your child's first teacher, use the opportunity of short trips
to start teaching him or her basic skills and concepts. Just open to a page for
one of the trips you plan to take today, skim through the easy step-by-step
instructions, and begin!

A WORD ABOUT SAFETY

Keep in mind that when doing the activities, an adult should supervise
to make sure that children do not place materials or objects in their mouths.
As for art materials, such as scissors, glue, or felt tip markers, use those that
are specifically labeled as safe for children unless the materials are to be used
only by an adult.

CONTENTS

MUSEUM

Dinosaurs

MUSEUM CHECKLIST

This prereading activity provides a fun plan for your museum visit.

1) Before going to the museum, talk with your child about the kinds of things you will see there.

2) With your child, make a picture list of five to eight items to look for. If an art museum is your destination, the list might include pictures of such things as a boat, a tree, a boy, and a girl. For a science museum, you might include a giant dinosaur and a butterfly exhibit on your list.

3) When you get to the museum, give your child the list and a pen.

4) Help your child check off the items on the list that you see as you walk through the museum.

TELL THE STORY

Help develop your child's imagination with this storytelling activity.

1) As you walk through the museum, look for a painting or exhibit that seems especially interesting to your child.

2) Ask your child if the painting or exhibit tells a story and if so, encourage him or her to tell it to you.

3) As your child tells the story, lead him or her to include details about what happened before and what will happen in the future.

4) Let your child choose a painting or exhibit for you to tell a story about.

POSTCARD MATCH

Use this matching activity to add something extra to your museum visit.

1) When you first arrive at the museum, visit the gift shop.

2) With your child, choose several postcards that have pictures of items that are on display at the museum.

3) Purchase the cards and give them to your child.

4) As you walk through the museum, have your child look for the items that are pictured on the postcards.

ANOTHER IDEA: For a problem-solving activity to do at home, cut each postcard into several interlocking pieces and let your child put the postcard puzzles back together.

STATUE

This movement activity will encourage your child's interest in what he or she sees at the museum.

1) When there are few people around, stop with your child in front of a statue or painting of a person or an exhibit of an animal.

2) Talk about how the person or animal is standing, sitting, or lying down.

3) Ask your child to assume the same pose and remain still like a statue for a few seconds.

4) Continue in the same manner with other paintings or exhibits.

VIEWING ART

Encourage your child's appreciation of art with this observation activity.

1) When you are viewing a painting with your child, ask questions such as the following.
   - "What colors do you see in the painting?"
   - "Can you see straight lines? Curved lines? Zigzag lines?"
   - "Can you find circles in the painting? Squares? Triangles?"
   - "If you could touch one thing in the painting, what would it be? How would it feel?"
   - "How does the painting make you feel?"

2) Continue with similar questions when viewing other paintings.

TOUR GUIDE

Try this dramatic-play activity after your child has experienced a guided museum tour.

1) Talk with your child about how a museum guide leads a group around and talks about what is on display.

2) Let your child pretend to be a guide and take you on a "tour" of your home.

3) Demonstrate by taking your child to the kitchen and saying something such as: "This is the kitchen. We make dinner here. We keep pots and pans in this cupboard and foods like milk and eggs in the refrigerator."

4) Have your child continue in the same manner.

ART EXHIBIT

You and your child can enjoy creating art together with this activity.

1) After a visit to an art museum, encourage your child to create art of his or her own.

2) If possible, provide art materials that are related to the kind of art you have just seen, such as watercolors, collage materials, or clay.

3) Join your child in using the materials to create paintings or sculptures.

4) Display your finished paintings on a wall and your sculptures on a table for family and friends to admire.

MAKING COLLECTIONS

This classification activity becomes meaningful after your child has made several museum visits.

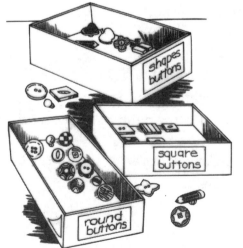

1) Talk with your child about different collections you have seen at a museum.

2) Encourage your child to make collections of such items as rocks, spoons, shoes, or buttons.

3) Help your child exhibit his or her collections on shelves or in open boxes.

4) Use index cards and a pen to print labels for the collections as your child dictates.

5) Encourage your child to change his or her collection exhibits every now and then.

ZOO

WHAT'S AT THE ZOO?

This activity uses prereading and prewriting skills.

1) Before you visit the zoo, check out several zoo picture books from the library.

2) Read the books with your child, helping him or her to learn the names of such animals as giraffes, hippos, camels, and flamingos.

3) With your child, make a picture list of three or four animals he or she would like best to see at the zoo.

4) On your zoo visit, give the list to your child and help him or her check off the animals as you see them.

ANOTHER IDEA: Let your child dictate questions he or she would like to ask a zookeeper. Take the questions with you when you and your child visit the zoo.

FOLLOW THE MAP

Try this easy prereading activity when you have no set plan for exploring the zoo.

1) Pick up a copy of the zoo map at the ticket window.

2) Show the map to your child and point out various animal areas.

3) Let your child close his or her eyes and point to a spot on the map.

4) When your child opens his or her eyes, follow the map to the area he or she pointed to.

ANOTHER IDEA: Take the map home and use it with your child to plot out future visits to the zoo.

ANIMAL SOUNDS

This activity is a great way to reinforce listening skills using a portable tape recorder.

1) Find a small portable tape recorder.

2) Carry the tape recorder with you when you visit the zoo.

3) As you walk by various animals, record the sounds they make.

4) Later, play back the tape and see if your child can identify each animal by its sound.

HINT: You may wish to write down the names of the animals in the order in which you record them to use as a guide while listening to the tape.

ANIMAL FAMILIES

This natural science activity uses classification skills.

1) At the zoo, choose a "family" of animals and visit several of its members. Here are some examples.

- Cat Family—Tigers, panthers, lions
- Ape Family—Monkeys, gorillas, chimpanzees
- Bear Family—Black bears, brown bears, polar bears
- Bird Family—Flamingos, parrots, peacocks
- Reptile Family—Snakes, lizards, alligators

2) As you visit each animal in a family, talk with your child about how it is like the other family members.

PETTING ZOO

This sensory-awareness activity uses vocabulary-building skills.

1) At the zoo, take your child to the petting zoo section.

2) Talk with your child about the different animals on display. (Most petting zoos include such animals as a cow, a goat, a pig, a chicken, and a rabbit.)

3) Encourage your child to pet the animals and talk about how they feel to the touch. Use such words as soft, silky, smooth, rough, bristly, and furry.

4) Look around for other textures for your child to explore; for example, a rough fence post, a prickly hay bale, or a smooth-sided pail.

LET'S PLAY ZOO

This dramatic-play activity is sure to spark your child's imagination.

1) Let your child make a pretend zoo in one or more rooms of your home.

2) Help your child use such items as furniture and pillows to set up special areas for different stuffed animals.

3) Have your child pretend to be the zookeeper, doing such tasks as "feeding" the animals and giving them "baths" with an imaginary hose.

4) If any of the animals get "sick," encourage your child to take the role of veterinarian and "treat" them.

5) When the animals are all taken care of, let your child pretend to be a guide and take you on a tour of the zoo.

AGE VARIATION: Help older children make a map of their pretend zoo.

ZOO RIDDLES

You and your child are sure to enjoy this problem-solving activity.

1) Recite the following riddles. Have your child guess the names of the animals.

- "I have a long tail. I live in trees. I like to eat bananas. Who am I?" (monkey)

- "I am gray. I have big ears. I have a long nose. Who am I?" (elephant)

- "I am king of the jungle. I have a golden mane. I like to roar. Who am I?" (lion)

- "I like to eat leaves. I have long legs. I have a very long neck. Who am I?" (giraffe)

- "I am white. I live where it is cold. I eat fish for my dinner. Who am I?" (polar bear)

2) Encourage your child to make up a simple Zoo Riddle for you to answer.

ZOO CHARADES

This problem-solving activity uses coordination skills.

1) With your child, look through a zoo picture book and talk about the different animals.

2) Invite your child to play a game of Zoo Charades.

3) Choose one of the animals, act out its movements, and ask your child to guess what animal it is.

4) Keep giving clues as necessary until your child guesses correctly.

5) Let your child choose a zoo animal and have you guess its name as he or she acts out its movements.

6) Continue taking turns playing the game as long as you wish.

PARK

SLIDE GAME

This simple experiment promotes predicting skills.

1) Take your child to the park playground.

2) Explain to your child that you are going to do a little experiment on the slide.

3) Show your child several items you have on hand, such as a ball, a pen, a rock, and a mitten.

4) Ask your child to predict which items will move down the slide the fastest and which will move down the slowest.

5) Have your child send the items down the slide and compare the results with his or her predictions.

PARK RUBBINGS

Increase your child's awareness of textures with this art activity.

1) When you visit the park, take along some old, peeled crayons and pieces of thin paper.

2) As you walk with your child, look for items that have surfaces of different textures, such as tree trunks, stones, leaves, cement pathways, or metal grillwork.

3) Show your child how to make a rubbing by placing a piece of paper on a textured surface and coloring over it with the side of a crayon.

4) Encourage your child to make as many different rubbings as he or she wishes.

5) When you return home, display your child's rubbings and talk about the textures they reveal.

SWING AND COUNT

This easy math activity provides fun for your child.

1) Find an empty swing for your child in the park playground.

2) When your child is seated in the swing, ask him or her to choose a number.

3) Push your child in the swing that number of times as he or she counts along with you.

4) When the swing stops moving, start the game again, if you wish.

MERRY-GO-ROUND WALK

You and your child will enjoy doing this whole-body movement activity.

1) Take your child to the park playground.

2) Sit opposite your child on the merry-go-round with your feet on the ground.

3) Ask your child to slowly "walk" the merry-go-round around in a circle with you.

4) Then ask your child to help you walk the merry-go-round quickly, with one foot, with the other foot, and so forth.

5) Encourage your child to think of other ways for you to walk the merry-go-round together.

NATURE COLLECTION

A park is a perfect place to find items for this natural science activity.

1) Give your child a paper bag to take along when you visit the park.

2) Let your child search for different nature items, such as seeds, leaves, pine cones, rocks, and bird feathers.

3) Have your child put the nature items he or she finds into the paper bag.

4) When you return home, help your child group the items by kind on a large piece of cardboard.

5) Below each group, write a simple label, such as "Seeds" or "Feathers."

6) Let your child add to his or her Nature Collection whenever he or she wishes.

ANOTHER IDEA: For a different kind of collecting activity, fasten a strip of masking tape sticky-side out around your child's wrist. Let your child attach small nature items he or she finds to the "bracelet."

LET'S PLAY PARK

Your child is sure to have fun creating his or her own park scene.

1) Let your child make a play park for small plastic people and animals.

2) Give your child a large green bath towel or piece of green fabric to arrange on the floor for a base.

3) Let your child make trees for the park by standing twigs in balls of modeling clay.

4) For a pond, have your child use a crayon to color a paper plate blue.

5) Encourage your child to add other items such as rocks or wood block "buildings."

6) Let your child act out scenes in his or her play park with the toy people and animals.

ANOTHER IDEA: With your child, make a pretend playground for stuffed animals that includes such things as a baking sheet slide, a scarf swing, a bookshelf climber, and a pan lid merry-go-round.

IN THE PARK OR NOT?

This sorting activity is a great way to reuse old magazines.

1) From magazines, cut pictures of people engaged in activities that might be done in a park, such as jogging, picnicking, playing on swings, wading in a pool, or observing birds.

2) Also cut out pictures of people engaged in activities that are not normally done in a park, such as vacuuming, baking cookies, brushing teeth, sleeping in a bed, or using a computer.

3) Mix up the pictures and place them in a pile.

4) Let your child sort the pictures into two groups: those that show activities people do in a park and those that show activities people do not do in a park.

HINT: For a more durable game, cover the magazine pictures with clear self-stick paper.

NATURE COLLAGE

This art activity provides a way to make use of extra nature items your child has collected at the park.

1) Set out small nature items and a bottle of glue.

2) Give your child a plastic-foam food tray that has been thoroughly washed and dried.

3) Let your child squeeze small amounts of glue onto the tray and place the nature items on top of the glue.

4) Encourage your child to continue until the entire tray is filled.

5) Let your child display his or her Nature Collage on a shelf or table.

AIRPORT

AIRPORT LEARNING

This prereading activity uses comparison skills.

1) Before your airport visit, find a picture book about airports.

2) Read the book to your child.

3) Use bookmarks to flag pictures that show several items to look for at the airport, such as the control tower, a jet plane, a person in uniform, and a cafeteria or snack bar.

4) Take the book with you when you and your child visit the airport.

5) As you come across each item that you flagged in the book, compare the item with the picture. Ask your child to tell you how they are alike and how they are different.

AIRPLANE STORY

Encourage your child to use his or her imagination when doing this storytelling activity.

1) At the airport, stand with your child where you can see an airplane with passengers starting to board.

2) Begin telling a story about how the plane will fly up into the sky with all its passengers.

3) Ask your child to continue the story, telling what the passengers will do and see on their journey.

4) To end the story say, "When it's time to land, what will the plane do? Where will the passengers go?"

5) Encourage your child to choose a different airplane to make up a new story about.

AIRPORT COUNTING

This activity promotes listening skills using an audio tape and a tape recorder.

1) As you walk through the airport, count with your child such things as those below.

   - number of people in uniforms
   - number of bags on a cart or carousel
   - number of airplanes on the tarmac

   - number of gates in a sequence

2) Encourage your child to look for more things to count.

ANOTHER IDEA: For a number-recognition game, name a number such as 3 and have your child search for it or listen for it over the loudspeaker.

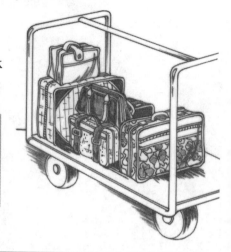

AIRPORT MATCHUPS

The airport provides many opportunities for using matching skills.

1) Stand with your child where you can see planes on the tarmac.

2) Talk with your child about how the planes are painted and what colors they are.

3) Ask your child to point to the matching-painted planes.

4) Continue by having your child look for other matchups, such as matching uniforms, matching-colored luggage, or matching kinds of foods displayed in a cafeteria or snack bar.

MOVING AROUND

This whole-body movement activity is easy and fun to do.

1) Talk with your child about how big the airport is.

2) Together, look for "people movers" that help people get around the airport quickly and easily, such as escalators, elevators, moving sidewalks, and subways.

3) Let your child choose one or two of the "people movers" to take a ride on.

4) As you ride together, talk about safety rules and demonstrate how to follow them.

AIRPLANE RIDE

This dramatic-play activity uses matching skills.

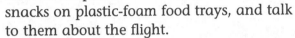

1) With your child, arrange chairs in rows to make an "airplane cabin."

2) Number paper squares in sequence and tape them to the chairs.

3) Write identical numbers on other paper squares to make "tickets" for stuffed-animal passengers.

4) While you play the role of pilot, let your child be the flight attendant and place the "passengers" in the matching-numbered seats.

5) When the plane "takes off," have the flight attendant do such things as hand out magazines to the passengers, serve them pretend snacks on plastic-foam food trays, and talk to them about the flight.

6) When the plane "lands," have the flight attendant help the passengers off the plane.

7) Trade places with your child and let him or her play the role of pilot.

DOES IT FLY?

Using classification skills is the focus of this sorting activity.

1) From old magazines, cut pictures of things that fly, such as an airplane, a butterfly, a bird, a balloon, and a helicopter; and pictures of things that do not fly, such as a car, a boat, a dog, a wagon, and a fish.

2) Glue the pictures on pieces of construction paper.

3) When the glue has dried, mix up the pictures and give them to your child.

4) Have your child sort the pictures into two groups—things that fly and things that do not fly.

PLASTIC-FOAM PLANE

Flying this play airplane promotes large-muscle development.

1) On a plastic-foam food tray, draw an airplane body shape, a wings shape, and a tail shape as shown in the illustration.

2) Cut out the shapes and make slits in the airplane body as indicated by the dotted lines.

3) Show your child how to insert the wings shape through the wide slit in the airplane body and the tail shape through the notched slit in the back.

4) Tape a penny to the nose section of the plane.

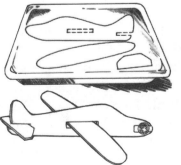

5) Let your child take the plane outdoors and have fun flying it in an open area.

ANOTHER IDEA:
For indoor play, let your child fly the plane around with his or her hand. You might wish to make a rule that when playing with toy airplanes, your child must be seated or kneeling.

PICNIC

PICNIC STORY BASKET

Try doing this storytelling activity while you are unpacking your picnic basket.

1) At the picnic site, invite your child to sit with you beside your picnic basket.

2) Start telling a picnic story and have your child take one item at a time out of the basket.

3) As your child does so, incorporate the items into your picnic story.

4) Continue the story until all the items have been removed from the basket.

ANOTHER IDEA: Let your child help you make up another story as you put items back into the picnic basket to take home.

FAMILY FAVORITES

Your child helps you plan a family picnic with this prereading-prewriting activity.

1) Before going on a picnic, let family members have a chance to contribute ideas.

2) With your child, make a list such as this: "Favorite Picnic Place, Favorite Picnic Food, Favorite Picnic Soft Drink, Favorite Picnic Activity, Favorite Friend to Invite."

3) Let your child ask each family member to name one or more "favorites" as you write the responses on the list.

4) Read through the completed list with your child.

5) Together, check off items on the list as you plan and prepare your family picnic.

PICNIC

Planning a picnic is the perfect time to try this letter-recognition activity.

1) Tell your child that you are going to have a *P* Picnic.

2) Together, tear out magazine pictures of foods with names that begin with P, such as peanut butter, pizza, popcorn, pretzels, pickles, peaches, pudding, and punch.

3) Let your child glue the pictures on paper to make a picture list.

4) Print the names of the foods next to the pictures and read over the list with your child.

5) Prepare a picnic lunch together, choosing from foods that are on your list.

6) Discuss the names of the P foods as you and your child enjoy your picnic.

I'LL BE THE GROWNUP

Use this activity to boost your child's self-esteem.

1) Plan to have a picnic for two with your child.

2) Before you go, switch roles with your child, letting him or her pretend to be the parent while you play the part of the child.

3) Let your child decide such things as where to go for your picnic, what time to leave, what foods to take, and what games to play.

4) Have your child continue playing the role of the parent while you enjoy your picnic together.

ANOTHER IDEA: Make clear ahead of time which decisions your child will be allowed to make when he or she is the parent.

COLOR PICNIC

Enjoy this color-recognition activity when just you and your child are going on a picnic.

1) With your child, choose a color for your picnic, such as green.

2) Decide together how you will incorporate green into your picnic, using ideas such as the following.

   - Wear green clothing.
   - Sit on green grass.
   - Eat green foods, such as grapes, celery, and pickles.
   - Take a walk to look for green things.

3) Talk about the color green as you and your child enjoy your picnic lunch.

INDOOR BEACH PICNIC

This dramatic-play activity is especially fun to do in wintertime.

1) Spread out a blanket or tablecloth on the floor.

2) Add beach items, such as shells, a beach ball, or a beach umbrella, if you wish.

3) With your child, dress for the beach, putting on such items as bathing suits or shorts, sandals, and sunglasses.

4) As you sit on your "beach blanket," serve a picnic of summer foods, such as melon balls, frozen yogurt, and iced drinks.

5) After your picnic, encourage your child to act out pretend beach activities.

BASKET PICKUP

This activity teaches letter-recognition skills.

1) Place a picnic basket on the floor.

2) Print the letter B on an index card and tape it to the basket.

3) Set out several objects with names that begin with B, such as a ball, a box, and a book, and several objects that begin with other letters.

4) Print the beginning letters of the objects on separate index cards and tape the cards to the objects.

5) Name the objects with your child and have him or her put those with names that begin with B into the picnic basket.

ANOTHER IDEA: Use other letters for this activity, such as P for picnic or L for lunch.

PICNIC ART

Your child is sure to enjoy this art activity.

1) With your child, tear pictures of "picnic" foods from old magazines.

2) Have your child glue the pictures onto a paper plate to make a "picnic" lunch.

3) For a tablecloth, give your child a large piece of paper, such as wrapping paper.

4) Let your child use a black ink pad to make fingerprint "ants" on the tablecloth.

5) Help your child glue or tape the paper plate to the tablecloth.

6) Let your child display his or her Picnic Art on a shelf or table.

FARM

FARM CHECKLIST

Use this prereading-prewriting activity to prepare your child for a visit to the farm.

1) Before going to the farm, make a picture list with your child of items to look for during your visit.

2) On your list, include such things as specific farm animals, an animal with a baby, an animal eating, a barn, a tractor, a pail, and a vegetable garden.

3) When you get to the farm, give your child the list and a pen.

4) As you walk through the farm, help your child check off items on the list that you see.

ACT IT OUT

This dramatic-play activity uses coordination skills.

1) As you walk around the farm, look for different tools and machines, such as shovels, rakes, pitchforks, pails, tractors, and trucks.

2) Point to a tool or machine and help your child name it.

3) Talk about how the tool or machine is used.

4) Have your child pretend to hold the tool or sit in the machine and act out how he or she would use it on the farm.

WHAT DID I SEE?

Your child is sure to enjoy this oral-language activity.

1) Take a notebook with you when you visit the farm.

2) On one of the pages, write a short story for your child such as the following: "One day I went to visit a farm. There were animals everywhere. The biggest animal I saw was a _____. The smallest animal I saw was a _____. The noisiest animals were the _____. The softest animals were the _____. The friendliest animals were the _____. If I could choose one animal to take home, I would choose the _____."

3) Later, read the story to your child and let him or her fill in the blanks as you write down his or her responses.

4) Let your child decorate the finished story with crayons or felt tip markers.

LET'S COMPARE

Try this comparison activity whenever it seems appropriate.

1) As you walk through the farm, help your child become aware of differences by asking questions such as the following.

- "How is a pig's nose different from a cow's nose?"
- "How is a horse's tail different from a pig's tail?"
- "How are a chicken's feet different from a goose's feet?"
- "How is a barn different from a house?"
- "How is animal food different from people food?"

2) Encourage your child to talk about other differences he or she observes.

MY OWN FARM BOOK

Take photos of your child at the zoo to use to make his or her own special book.

1) When you visit the farm, take along a camera.

2) Snap pictures of your child in various places around the farm and with different animals.

3) Later, when the photographs have been developed, glue them in a blank book in an order that tells a story.

4) Write the story, using simple sentences, underneath the photos.

5) Read the book with your child, encouraging him or her to add more details as you look at the pictures.

6) Suggest that your child "read" his or her book to other members of the family.

Brighter Vision Publications 18 BV15012 Teaching Trips

FARMYARD MURAL

You and your child will enjoy doing this creative art activity.

1) Lay a piece of large paper or cardboard on the floor.

2) On the paper, use felt tip markers to draw a simple farm scene that includes such things as a barn, a fence, and a tree.

3) With your child, look through old magazines and tear or cut out pictures of farm animals.

4) Let your child glue the animal pictures on the paper to complete the Farmyard Mural.

5) Display the mural on a wall for everyone to admire.

ANOTHER IDEA: Draw a farmyard scene on a piece of construction paper. Let your child add farm animal stickers or stamp on farm animal pictures with rubber stamps.

FARM ANIMAL SOUNDS

This activity promotes listening and oral-language skills.

1) Find a farm animal picture book.

2) Look at the pictures with your child and talk about the sound each animal makes.

3) Make up a story about farm animals and tell it to your child.

4) Whenever your child hears the name of an animal, have him or her make that animal's sound.

ANOTHER IDEA: For a different kind of farm animal sounds activity, sing "Old MacDonald Had a Farm" with your child.

MOTHERS AND BABIES

Vocabulary building is the focus of this language activity.

1) Check your local library for a picture book of farm animals and their babies.

2) Look through the book with your child.

3) As you do so, teach your child the names for farm animal babies such as these: cow–calf, sheep–lamb, pig–piglet, chicken–chick, horse–colt, duck–duckling, goat–kid, goose–gosling.

WOODS

NATURE SORT

Nature provides great materials to use for this sorting activity.

1) Carrying a bag or other container, take your child on a walk through the woods.

2) Together, collect nature items, such as leaves, pine cones, twigs, and stones, and place them in the bag.

3) When you return from your walk, let your child empty the bag and sort the items by kind into separate piles.

MINIATURE CAMPSITE

Your child uses rocks for "dolls" in this creative-play activity.

1) When you are camping, help your child collect nature items in the woods.

2) Let your child create a miniature campsite using the nature items; for example, a leaf could be used for a fire pit, twigs might be arranged as a tent, and moss could serve as a lake or stream.

3) Have your child select rocks to represent members of a family.

4) Let your child play with the rock people in his or her miniature campsite.

IS IT LITTER?

This classification activity helps your child understand what litter is.

1) When you are camping with your child, talk about the importance of keeping the woods free of litter.

2) On a tray, place several litter items, such as a plastic bag, an empty soft drink can, a scrap of paper, and a gum wrapper; and several nature items, such as a pine cone, a leaf, a feather, and a stone.

3) Explain to your child that litter is garbage that has not been put into a trash can.

4) Talk about the items on the tray and help your child divide them into two groups: litter items and nonlitter items.

5) Have your child throw the litter items into a trash can and place the nature items back on the ground.

ANOTHER IDEA:
Talk with your child about how litter left in the woods can be harmful to the animals who live there. For instance, the animals could get caught in plastic six-pack rings, get cut by rusted cans, or become sick from eating garbage.

NATURE PATTERNS

Try using various kinds of nature items for this patterning activity.

1) Collect a number of small twigs and stones.

2) Clear a space on the ground for you and your child to sit.

3) In front of you, arrange several twigs and stones in a row in a pattern such as twig-stone-twig-stone.

4) Invite your child to use more twigs and stones to continue the pattern.

5) Repeat, arranging the items in various patterns for your child to continue.

6) Let your child create a pattern for you to repeat.

CAMPING COMPARISONS

Try this comparison activity any time you are camping.

1) Ask your child to tell you how activities such as the ones below are done differently when camping than they are at home.
   - cooking
   - eating meals
   - sleeping
   - washing
   - dressing
   - playing

2) Which ways of doing things does your child like better? Why?

LET'S PLAY CAMP

Your child will have fun "camping" with this dramatic-play activity.

1) Create a campsite at home for your child to play in.

2) Set up a tent with a sleeping bag inside and put out several camp stools or chairs.

3) Move a small table to a spot near the tent and place camping cookware and eating utensils on it.

4) Help your child arrange rocks in a circle for a pretend fire pit.

5) Let your child play in the campsite, doing such things as cooking pretend meals, exploring the "woods" with a flashlight, and napping inside the tent.

WHEN I GO CAMPING

This memory game is always fun to play.

1) Arrange sticks in a pile to make a pretend campfire.

2) Sit by the "fire" with your child.

3) Take turns saying, "When I go camping, I always take my _____."

4) As each of you takes a turn, repeat all the items mentioned from the beginning of the game before adding a new item.

AGE VARIATION: For younger children, start the game over frequently so that the list of items does not become too long to remember.

TRAIL SNACK

Making this portable snack helps promote small-muscle development.

1) Give your child a long piece of string with a large knot tied in one end and the other end taped to make a "needle."

2) Set out a bowl of O-shaped cereal pieces.

3) Let your child thread the cereal pieces onto the string.

4) When your child finishes, tie the ends of the string around his or her neck.

5) Let your child enjoy his or her necklace snack while exploring "trails" around a backyard campsite.

BEACH

SAND MOLDS
Your child will have fun with this creative-play activity.

1) When you go to the beach, take along a bag filled with sturdy containers, such as plastic measuring cups, plastic food tubs of various sizes, and small gelatin molds.

2) Let your child pack the containers full of wet sand, turn them over, and then remove the containers to reveal the molded sand shapes.

3) Encourage your child to create "cakes," a "house," or whatever else he or she chooses.

HINT: Use a mesh bag, such as a citrus bag, to carry the containers. When you are ready to go home, just rinse the bag of containers with fresh water to wash away the sand.

SHELL LINEUP
This ordering activity involves counting skills.

1) As you walk along the beach with your child, pick up different sizes of shells.

2) Have your child help smooth out an area in the sand.

3) Give the shells to your child and let him or her line them up on the sand from smallest to largest or from largest to smallest.

4) Count the number of shells with your child.

ANOTHER IDEA: Use small stones instead of shells.

BEACH BLANKET FUN

Your child uses sensory clues in this predicting activity.

1) Spread out a blanket at the beach.

2) While your child closes his or her eyes, hide a familiar object, such as a ball or a sand shovel, under the blanket.

3) When your child opens his or her eyes, let him or her touch the object through the blanket and try to guess what it is.

4) After your child responds, have him or her look under the blanket to see if the guess was correct.

5) Let your child hide an object under the blanket and have you guess what it is.

BURIED TREASURE

Digging for treasure encourages large-muscle development.

1) Find a pretty shell or rock on the beach.

2) Let your child help you make a large mound in the sand.

3) While your child closes his or her eyes, hide the shell or rock in the sand mound.

4) Have your child open his or her eyes and dig through the sand to find the "treasure."

5) Let your child bury the shell or rock in a mound of sand for you to find.

SAND TOYS

Playing with these homemade toys encourages large-muscle development.

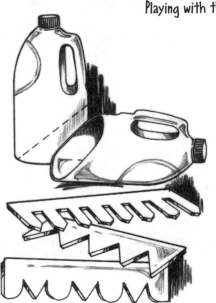

1) Before going to the beach, make the toys below.

   • Sand Scoop—Wash and dry an empty bleach bottle and screw the cap back on tightly. Cut off the bottom of the bottle diagonally to make a scoop with a handle.

   • Sand Combs—Cut heavy cardboard into rectangles about 6 by 12 inches. On one of the long sides of each rectangle, cut several notches, varying the shapes and sizes of the notches on each rectangle.

2) At the beach, let your child dig with the sand scoop and make patterns in the sand with the sand combs.

FOLLOW THE TRAIL

Your child will enjoy this whole-body movement activity.

1) Find a smooth, sandy area at the beach.

2) With a stick, draw a long, straight line in the sand and have your child walk along it.

3) Continue drawing various kinds of lines for your child to follow—lines that curve, lines that zigzag, lines that stop and start, or lines that go round in circles.

4) Let your child use the stick to draw lines for you to follow.

COLLECTING JAR

This natural science activity helps your child make the decision of what to take home from the beach.

1) When you go to the beach, take along a plastic jar with a lid.

2) Give the jar to your child, explaining that he or she can take home any nonliving beach items, such as empty shells, rocks, or sticks, that will fit in the jar.

3) Encourage your child to take his or her time choosing just what he or she wants to keep.

4) When you return home, fill the remainder of the jar with water, add a few drops of bleach to keep the water fresh, and screw the lid on tightly.

5) Let your child display the jar on a table or shelf.

UNDERWATER VIEWER

Your child uses observation skills with this natural science activity.

1) Before leaving home, make a viewer for your child to use at the beach.

2) Cut the middle section out of a large, plastic soft-drink bottle.

3) Cover one end of the section with plastic wrap and secure it with a large rubber band.

4) At the beach, show your child how to use the viewer to observe underwater scenes in a tide pool.

5) Stay with your child, encouraging him or her to describe what he or she sees through the viewer.

BACKYARD BEACH

Try this dramatic-play activity on a warm summer day.

1) Create a make-believe beach in your yard.

2) Set out one tub of sand and another of water.

3) Add some shells to the sand tub and a few plastic fish to the water tub.

4) Give your child beach items such as sand scoops and funnels, a string "fishing line," a large beach towel, sunglasses, a sun hat, and a small portable radio.

5) Let your child play at the pretend beach, doing such things as digging in the sand, "fishing" in the water, and relaxing in the sun.

MAKING WAVES

This homemade toy will provide your child with hours of creative fun.

1) Find a plastic jar with a lid.

2) Fill the jar two-thirds full of water.

3) Add several drops of blue food coloring and mix well.

4) Fill up the rest of the jar with mineral oil, getting rid of as many air bubbles as possible.

5) Secure the lid of the jar with strong glue.

6) Let your child hold the jar sideways and gently tip it back and forth to make "waves."

FISH PUPPET

A fish puppet makes this storytelling activity fun to do.

1) Use a business-size envelope to make a fish puppet.

2) Tuck in the flap of the envelope.

3) Put your hand inside the envelope with your fingers at one end and your thumb at the other.

4) Indent the middle of the envelope toward your hand and fold your fingers and thumb together to make the puppet.

5) Use felt tip markers to draw on eyes, scales, and fins.

6) Open and close your hand to make the puppet "talk" as you tell your child a fish story.

TRAVEL GAMES

MAP FUN

Your child is sure to enjoy this prereading activity.

1) Before going on a trip, draw a simple map that shows familiar landmarks you will be passing on your way.

2) When you get in the car, give your child the map and a pen.

3) Have your child use the pen to check off each landmark on the map as you pass it.

ANOTHER IDEA: If your destination is a frequent one, cover the map with clear self-stick paper and let your child check off the familiar landmarks with a black crayon. At the end of the trip, just wipe off the crayon marks with a dry cloth and the map will be ready to use again.

LOOKING FOR LETTERS

Reviewing the alphabet is the focus of this letter-recognition activity.

1) As you are riding in the car, choose an alphabet letter such as B.

2) Point out one or two B's you see in road signs.

3) Ask your child to look for more B's as you are traveling.

4) To start a new game, choose another letter to search for.

5) Continue the game as long as interest lasts.

AGE VARIATION: Ask older children to search for letters that spell their names.

COOKIE TIN MAGNETBOARD

Magnets provide the fun in this creative-play activity.

1) Find a cookie tin with a lid.

2) Collect decorative kitchen magnets and place them inside the cookie tin.

3) Take the tin with you when you go on a trip.

4) Let your child use the cookie tin lid as a magnetboard, arranging and rearranging the magnets on it any way he or she wishes.

QUIET GAME

Try this observation game when the noise level gets too high in your car.

1) Select an item that you are not likely to see often when traveling, such as a cement mixer or a yellow car with three people in it.

2) Ask your child to use only a "whisper voice" until he or she sees that item.

3) When the item is sighted, let your child resume talking in a normal voice.

4) To start a new game, choose another unfamiliar item and ask your child to look for it.

AGE VARIATION: For younger children, choose a common item to make the game shorter, and for older children, choose a less common item to make the game longer.

WHAT GOES WITH IT?

This classification game is fun to play in the car.

1) Name an item that usually is associated with another object and have your child name its partner.

2) Use examples such as these: salt–pepper, knife–fork, shoes–socks, soap–water, toothbrush–toothpaste.

3) Accept any answer that has an association of any kind.

PICTURE THIS

Use this storytelling activity to stimulate your child's imagination.

1) Cut interesting pictures out of old magazines.

2) When you are going on a trip in the car, tape one of the pictures where your child can see it while sitting in his or her car seat or seat belt.

3) Ask your child to describe the picture.

4) Together, make up a story about the picture, pausing often to let your child tell what happens next.

5) Keep a supply of pictures in your car and change them often on long trips.

TRAVEL BOX

This travel toy can be stored in the car and used almost anywhere to promote creative play.

1) Find a plastic storage box, about 8 by 13 by 3 inches, with a lid.

2) Inside the box, store such items as a notepad, crayons, stickers, card games, and small plastic toys.

3) Let your child use the lid of the box as a "table" for drawing, playing games, or playing with toys.

LACING CARD

Promoting small-muscle development is the focus of this activity.

1) Find a greeting card made out of stiff paper.

2) Cut off the front of the card, discarding the back.

3) Use a hole punch to punch holes about 1 inch apart around the edges of the card front.

4) Tie one end of a long piece of yarn through one of the holes.

5) Wrap the other end of the yarn piece with tape to make a "needle."

6) Give the card to your child and let him or her lace the yarn around it through the holes.

7) Unlace the yarn and let your child lace it around the card again.

NUMBER GAMES

These math games help make travel time pass more quickly.

1) When riding in the car with your child, try one or more of the following ideas.

   - Have your child look for a particular number, such as his or her age or the day's date.

   - Choose a number such as 3. On a short trip, see how many 3s you and your child can "collect" from road signs and license plates.

   - Mentally choose an object to count, such as motorcycles, busses, or red cars. Each time you see one of the objects, count out loud. Have your child try to guess what you are counting.

- Select a category of items to count, such as supermarkets, vans, or billboards. With your child, see who can count the highest number of items in 10 minutes.

2) Let your child choose items he or she would like to count.

BRAINTEASERS

This car game promotes problem-solving skills.

1) In a notebook, make short lists of Brainteasers for your child to respond to, such as the following.

   - "How is a glove like your hand?"

   - "Can you put your elbow in your ear?"

   - "Can a cow really jump over the moon?"

- "Name one thing you can see in the sky at night."

- "Name one thing you can see in the sky in the morning."

2) Each time you go on a trip, select one of the Brainteaser lists, read the entries to your child, and have him or her respond.

COLOR GAMES

These color-recognition games are great car activities.

1) With your child, try one or more of the following ideas.

   - Call out a color name and type of vehicle such as, "Blue station wagon!" See which of you can spot the first one.

   - Choose a color and take turns with your child naming things that are that color.

   - Select a color you see inside the car and have your child name something outside the car that is the same color.

   - Choose an item and have your child look for items that are the same color; for example, if you choose a pickle, have your child look for green items.

2) Encourage your child to think of other color games to play.

TRIP TIPS

BEFORE YOU GO

BEST TIME
Choose the best time to visit the site. For instance, go to a museum early in the day to avoid crowds. Visit the zoo at feeding time. Take your child to an ocean beach at low tide. Avoid an airport visit during the busy holiday season.

PLAN AHEAD
Familiarize yourself with the location ahead of time, if possible, and make sure that any tour you plan to take is appropriate. Keep in mind that young children enjoy seeing and touching things they can identify with and understand.

CALENDAR COUNTDOWN
To help your child figure out the number of days before your planned outing, first attach a sticker to the date of the outing on a calendar. Then starting with today's date, let your child mark off each day with a crayon and count to see how many days remain.

WHAT TO TAKE

MATCHING T-SHIRTS
If you are going to a place where there will be a lot of people, dress your child in a T-shirt that matches yours in color or design. That way, he or she can easily spot you in a crowd.

CAMERA AND TAPE RECORDER
Take a camera and a tape recorder (or a video camera) with you on outings. Later, you can use the photos and recorded tapes to review what your child experienced.

SNACKTIME
Pack snack foods, such as raisins, pretzels, small crackers, and fruit chunks, in sections of an empty egg carton. Your child can sample the snacks in the car or at the site.

EMERGENCY BOX
For minor emergencies on outings, take along a box containing such things as facial tissues, small bandages, rubber bands, safety pins, and disposable wipes.

SONG TAPES
Take tape recordings of favorite songs to play in the car. If your child gets restless, put on a tape and encourage him or her to sing along.

ON THE WAY

TAKE A BREAK
Before going on an outing, estimate the time it will take to get to the site. If it is more than half an hour, plan to take a break about halfway there.

ACTIVE TIME
Plan an active time before your visit if your child is expected to be quiet at the location. Schedule a restroom stop before arriving.

SCENIC ROUTE
If possible, take a scenic route when you go on an outing so that you can point out things of interest to your child along the way. This will help travel time pass more quickly.

TRIP TIPS

AT THE SITE

LIMIT YOUR TIME
Don't spend too much time at the location. A half hour to one hour is usually long enough for young children.

KEEP THINGS SIMPLE
On an outing, avoid confusing your child by calling attention to every new thing in sight. Instead, help him or her concentrate on three or four things that are of interest.

POINTING THINGS OUT
When you are pointing out something to your child, kneel down so that you are at his or her level. This allows you to help your child better understand what he or she is observing.

UP FRONT
When you are in a group with a tour guide, try standing in the front rather than in back. Children often are more quiet when they can really see and hear what is going on. Remind your child to "listen quietly to the person's story."

ENJOY IT ALL
Take time to enjoy with your child what may seem to you to be irrelevant. For instance, four flights of stairs in a row might be a wonderful mountain in your child's eyes. Fancy water fountains may require stops. Eating at a cafeteria or putting money in the parking meter might be the highlight of the outing. Having a positive experience together should be your goal.

WHEN YOU RETURN

WHAT DID WE DO?
Be sure to recall the outing with your child by reminding him or her about what you did. For a simple recall game, take turns repeating the sentence, "I saw a _____."

DRAMATIC PLAY
Set up play situations that encourage your child to reenact outings that you have taken. You'll find that your child enjoys using the information he or she has learned.

MAKING A DISPLAY
When you get back from an outing, display pictures and souvenirs of the trip and talk about them with your child. This will help keep the fun alive.

KEEPING A JOURNAL
Keep a blank notebook, along with crayons and felt tip markers, in your car. Your child can draw pictures of your outings in it and dictate sentences for you to add. Later, photocopy the pages and send them to family members as letters, or use them to make a book for your child to "read."

FAMILY MEMBERSHIP
After visiting a place that you really enjoy, such as a museum or zoo, consider investing in a family membership. That way, you and your child can go often for short visits without feeling that you have to "get your money's worth" each time.

PHOTO FUN
When your photos of an outing have been developed, let your child help put them into a special album. Encourage him or her to dictate captions for you to write under the photos.